Workbook

for Inner City Youths with Severe Behavioral Problems

A Tool for Engaging Young People

Written by: Hugh Alexis, MSW, LCSW-C

Illustrated by Lauren Bauman

Edited by James Stimson

Published by CreateSpace, USA

Table of Contents

Introduction

This workbook was compiled with a series of activities created over the years while practicing clinical social work treatment with individuals and families in Baltimore City. The activities specifically target some of the re-occurring themes which surface when treating inner city youths. The therapeutic activities, however, can be used with any youth presenting the challenges covered in the workbook. Children and adolescents from any geographical location or from any racial or ethnic group may benefit from doing the activities in the book. Please note that the activities alone are insufficient to foster change in the targeted population group. The research indicates that young people make positive change in treatment when they feel that the treatment provider is genuine and interested in their lives and their treatment.

It is highly recommended that the workbook be used by a clinician; however, para-professionals and non-judgmental parents and or caregivers may also use the workbook with young people so as to engage them in dialogue about their challenges.

When using the material in the book, ask a series of open ended questions. The activities can be given as assignments to complete during the session, or they can be prescribed as homework assignments.

The excerpts used in the workbook are real stories shared by previous clients. The names of the clients were changed. The stories are kept short so as to not bore the client and lose his or her interest. Some youths may experience difficulties reading and understanding the materials, and in such cases the clinician should offer to explain the material to the client. If the clinician assess that the patient cannot read, he or she should read the questions to the patient in a non-pejorative manner, explore their response, and if possible, record the answers in the workbook.

When treating inner city adolescents, it is important set clearly defined boundaries, yet, it is also important to be flexible and give the patient some autonomy over his or her own treatment. You may want to say that, "It is important for us to meet at least once a week, but I know that from time to time you may not want to see me, when this occurs please call me at least 2 or 3 hours in advance to let me know that you want to be excused from therapy for that day. I promise that I won't be upset."

For questions in using the material in the workbook, I can be reached at hughalexis@yahoo.com.

The book was written by Hugh Alexis, LCSW-C.

Edited by James Stimson.

Illustrated and formatted by Lauren Bauman.

In the box below, draw a picture of yourself prior to your behavior problems surfacing.

```



```

How old are you in the picture?

_____

Is there anything about this age you like? Explain.

_____

_____

_____

What, if anything, didn't you like about this age?

_____

_____

_____

What activities did you enjoy doing at this age?

_____

_____

_____

What was your relationship like with your parents/caregivers at this age? Explain.

_____

_____

_____

In the box below draw a picture of how you look currently.

```




```

How is this picture different from your previous picture?

_____

_____

_____

What, if anything, do you like about your current age? Explain.

_____

_____

_____

Is there anything about being this age that you don't like? Explain.

_____

_____

_____

What kinds of activities interest you at this age? Explain.

_____

_____

_____

How is your relationship with your parents different at this age as compared to your relationship with your parents in the previous picture? Explain.

_____

_____

_____

In the box below, draw a picture of yourself with some of your closest friends.

```
┌─────────────────────────────────────────────┐
│                                             │
│                                             │
│                                             │
│                                             │
│                                             │
│                                             │
│                                             │
│                                             │
│                                             │
│                                             │
│                                             │
│                                             │
│                                             │
│                                             │
│                                             │
│                                             │
│                                             │
│                                             │
└─────────────────────────────────────────────┘
```

What is happening in the picture? Explain.

_____

_____

_____

Name the friends you depicted in the picture.

_____

Which friend is most positive? Explain.

_____

_____

_____

Which friend is most negative, or just a little negative? Explain.

_____

_____

_____

Friendships

In the previous activity you named negative and a positive friend.

How might your positive friend influence you positively? Explain.

_____
_____
_____
_____
_____
_____

What do you like about this friend? Explain.

_____
_____
_____
_____
_____
_____

How might the negative friend you named influence you negatively, even if it is just a little negative? Explain.

_____
_____
_____
_____
_____

What do you like about this friend? Explain.

_____
_____
_____
_____
_____

If you were a parent, which of the friends you mentioned would you ask your child to avoid being around, or to be careful when being around that individual? If none, explain your reason.

_____
_____
_____
_____
_____

Oppositional Behaviors

Some young people experience difficulties following reasonable directions from adult authority figures at home, school, and/or in the community.

Do you experience difficulties following reasonable directions?   Yes   No

Where do you experience the most difficulties following directions?

Home   School   Community

I experience severe difficulties following directions at/in: _____

Explain:

_____
_____
_____
_____
_____

I experience moderate difficulties following directions at/in: _____

Explain:

_____
_____
_____
_____
_____

I experience mild difficulties directions at/in: _____

Explain:

_____
_____
_____
_____
_____

Fighting

Have you gotten into any physical fights with a child or adult within the past year?

Yes   No

If you had a fight, who started the fight? _____

Explain what happened.

_____

_____

_____

_____

Have you ever been told by a peer or an adult that you start most of the fights you are involved in?   Yes   No

What have you been told? Explain.

_____

_____

_____

Do you believe there is anything true about what you were told? Explain.

_____

_____

_____

What do you think is not true about what you have been told? Explain.

_____

_____

_____

What are three negative implications of fighting?

1. _____

_____

2. _____

_____

3. _____

_____

How do you feel after a fight? Explain.

_____

_____

_____

Stealing

Have you ever taken things from someone without permission or have you ever taken things from a business place such as a store without paying?   Yes   No

What have you taken?

_____

_____

_____

Who or where have you taken things from?

_____

_____

_____

What about the item you took made you want to take it? Explain.

_____

_____

_____

Do you feel like you did something wrong by taking this item or do you feel justified? Explain.

_____

_____

_____

Has anyone ever taken something from you?   Yes   No

Explain what happened.

_____

_____

_____

_____

What did it feel like to have something taken away from you without your permission? Explain.

_____

_____

_____

How did you deal with the situation? Explain.

_____

_____

_____

Animal Cruelty

Some people become very upset with others and they take their anger out on animals. Other people simply get pleasure from inflicting pain on animals.

Have you ever hurt an animal?   Yes   No

Maybe you have never hurt an animal before, but has anyone ever accused you of hurting an animal?   Yes   No

What animal did you hurt or what animal were you accused of hurting?

_____

What about this animal made you hurt it?

_____
_____
_____
_____

What were you feeling while you were hurting this animal, for example (happy, justified, angry)? Explain your feelings.

_____
_____
_____
_____

Is there something about this animal that you do not like? Explain.

_____
_____
_____
_____

What about this animal may other people like? Explain.

_____
_____
_____
_____

Animal Cruelty Continued

Three animals are listed below. For each animal, write 3 good things and 3 not so good things about each animal.

Dogs

Positive things:

1. _____
2. _____
3. _____

Negative things:

1. _____
2. _____
3. _____

Cats

Positive things:

1. _____
2. _____
3. _____

Negative things:

1. _____
2. _____
3. _____

Birds

Positive things:

1. _____
2. _____
3. _____

Negative things:

1. _____
2. _____
3. _____

Robbery

Have you ever been involved in a robbery?   Yes   No

Have you ever been wrongfully accused of robbing someone?   Yes   No

When was the last time you robbed someone or was accused of robbing someone? Explain.

_____
_____
_____

If you robbed someone, explain what happened, or if you were accused of robbing someone explain what the accuser, or the police said you did?

_____
_____
_____

What was going through you mind before you robbed this individual?

_____
_____
_____

What was going through your mind while you were robbing this individual?

_____
_____
_____

Maybe you have never robbed someone, what do you think goes through a young person's mind when he/she robbing someone?

_____
_____
_____

How did you feel after you robbed that individual, or how do you think other people feel after a robbery? Explain.

_____
_____
_____

In your opinion, what do you think is the reason for young people committing robberies?

_____
_____
_____

Gun Violence

Have you ever come into physical contact with a firearm?   Yes   No

How old were you when you first came into contact with a gun/firearm?

_____

What feelings did you experience when you first came into contact with a gun? For example, excited, scared, powerful. Explain.

_____
_____
_____

Have you ever used a gun to shoot someone?   Yes   No

Explain what happened.

_____
_____
_____

Do you plan on using a gun in the future?   Yes   No

You may not be planning to use a gun in the future, but would you feel comfortable using a gun in the future? Explain.

_____
_____
_____

Is there anything about guns that you like or don't like? Explain.

_____
_____
_____

In the USA, many young people are involved in gun violence. In your opinion, what is the reason for this? Explain.

_____
_____
_____

In your opinion, how might gun violence be stopped or minimized? Explain.

_____
_____
_____

Gang Involvement

Are you a member of any negative peer group or gang?   Yes   No

Have you ever been accused by any family member of being a member of a gang or a negative peer group?   Yes   No

Do you have any friends who are members of negative peer groups or gangs?   Yes   No

If you or your friend(s) are members of negative peer groups or gangs, explain how you or your friend(s) benefit from being a gang member.

_____
_____
_____
_____
_____

Do you know of anyone who has benefited as a result of being a gang member? Explain.

_____
_____
_____

Have you or anyone you know encountered problems as a result of being a gang member?

_____
_____
_____

Do you have any fears or concerns about either you or your friend(s) being a member of a negative peer group or gang?

_____
_____
_____

Do you ever feel like discontinuing your gang membership?   Yes   No

What are your fears, if any, about discontinuing your gang membership?

_____
_____
_____

Drug use

Have you ever smoked cigarettes?   Yes   No

How old were you when you first smoked cigarettes? _____

When was the last time you smoked cigarettes? _____

Have you ever drank alcohol?   Yes   No

How old were you when you first used alcohol? _____

When was the last time you used alcohol? _____

Have you ever used marijuana or other mind-altering substances?   Yes   No

How old were you when you first used marijuana or other mind-altering substances? _____

When was the last time you used marijuana or other mind-altering substances? _____

If you use marijuana, do you use it alone or do you use it with friends? Explain.

_____

_____

_____

How do you get access to this substance? Do you buy it or do your friends share their drugs with you? Explain.

_____

_____

_____

What about this substance do you like?

_____

_____

_____

_____

How do you feel before you use this substance?

_____

_____

_____

How do you feel after you use this substance? Explain.

_____

_____

_____

Drug Use Continued

How often do you use this substance? Explain.

_____

_____

Have you ever thought of discontinuing your drug use?   Yes   No

Explain.

_____

_____

_____

Are you at a point in your drug use where you feel like you need to use it several times a day or a week? Explain.

_____

_____

_____

Does your drug use affect your relationship with others, your performance at school, your job or your behavior in the community?   Yes   No

How does your drug use affect your relationship with your:

Parents? Explain.

_____

_____

_____

School? Explain.

_____

_____

_____

Employment? Explain.

_____

_____

_____

Community? Explain.

_____

_____

_____

Drug Sale

Have you ever sold drugs or been accused of selling drugs?   Yes   No

Explain.

_____

_____

Who accused you or made comments about your involvement in selling drugs? Explain.

_____

_____

In your opinion, what do you think caused that individual to make that accusation against you?

Explain.

_____

_____

_____

Is there anything about selling drugs which interests you? Explain.

_____

_____

_____

If you are involved in selling drugs, is there anything about selling drugs which concerns you, or makes you uncomfortable? Explain.

_____

_____

_____

Have you ever gotten in trouble with the law for selling drugs? Explain what happened.

_____

_____

_____

Have you ever thought of discontinuing selling drugs? Explain.

_____

_____

_____

What makes you think about continuing to sell drugs or discontinuing selling drugs?

_____

_____

_____

Sex

Some young people act out sexually for a variety of reasons.

Are you sexually active?   Yes   No

How old were you when you first had consensual sex? _____

Did you first have consensual sex with a male or a female? _____

How did it happen?

Explain.

_____

_____

_____

Do you engage in safe sex practices?   Yes   No

What does safe sex mean to you? Explain.

_____

_____

_____

What safe sex practices do you use? Explain.

_____

_____

_____

What do you like about sex?

_____

_____

_____

Is there any potential negative impact on your life from engaging in sex? For example, does it affect your functioning at school, home and/ or in the community?

_____

_____

_____

Do you have any concerns about being a young single parent? Explain.

_____

_____

_____

Problems at School

Do you ever get into trouble at school?   Yes   No

Explain.

_____
_____
_____

Have you ever been suspended from school?   Yes   No

When was the last time you were suspended from school? Explain.

_____
_____
_____

What was the reason for you being suspended from school the last time you were suspended?
Explain.

_____
_____
_____

How do you get along with most of your teachers at school? Explain.

_____
_____
_____

How do you get along with most of your classmates? Explain.

_____
_____
_____

What do you like about school?

    1. _____
    2. _____
    3. _____

What don't you like about school?

    1. _____
    2. _____
    3. _____

Truancy

Truancy is a common problem experienced by many young people. There may be several factors contributing to truancy.

Do you fail to attend school daily and on time?   Yes   No

Explain.

_____

_____

_____

What factor(s) contribute(s) to your truancy? Explain.

_____

_____

_____

Do you experience any problems at school which contribute to your truancy? Explain.

_____

_____

_____

Do you ever feel tense and nervous when you are at school? Explain.

_____

_____

_____

Do you feel that attending school can make your adult life better? Explain.

_____

_____

_____

Is school important or unimportant to you? Explain.

_____

_____

_____

What action can you take to improve your school attendance? Explain.

_____

_____

_____

How may others help you or encourage you to attend school? Explain.

_____

_____

Living with Parents/Step-Parent

Some children live with their biological parents, others live with step-parents, and/or blended families.

Who do you live with, or how would you describe your household? Explain.

_____

_____

_____

How do you get along with your parent(s) or caregiver(s)? Explain.

_____

_____

_____

On a scale of 1 to 10, rate how you get along with your parent(s) or caregiver(s).

_____

1   2   3   4   5   6   7   8   9   10

What about your parent(s) or caregiver(s) do you like?

1. _____

2. _____

3. _____

What about your parent(s) or caregiver(s) don't you like?

1. _____

2. _____

3. _____

What can you do to have a better relationship with your parent(s) or caregiver(s)? Explain.

_____

_____

_____

_____

What can your parent(s) or caregiver(s) do to have a better relationship with you? Explain.

_____

_____

_____

_____

Living in Foster Care, Group Home, Residential Care

In what setting do you currently live? Explain.

_____

_____

_____

How long have you been living in this setting?

_____

What happened that caused you to live in this setting?

_____

_____

_____

Since being removed from your primary family, how many placements have you had so far?

_____

_____

_____

What has your experience been like in this placement? Explain.

_____

_____

_____

Explain two things you like about your current placement.

    1. _____

    _____

    2. _____

    _____

Explain two things you do not like about this placement.

    1. _____

    _____

    2. _____

    _____

If you could change one thing about your current placement, what would that be? Explain.

_____

_____

_____

_____

In the box below, draw a picture of your biological family or the family you would like to live with.

```



```

What do you like about this family?

_____
_____
_____

What don't you like about this family?

_____
_____
_____

Is there a possibility that you can return, or be placed in this family?   Yes   No

Explain in your own words what needs to happen so that you can return to this family.

_____
_____
_____
_____

Going Out Privileges

Does your parent(s) or caregiver(s) give you going out privileges? Explain.

_____
_____
_____
_____

In your own words, explain your understanding of your parent(s) giving you or refusing to give you going out privileges?

_____
_____
_____
_____

List and explain 4 reasons a parent may not grant going out privileges.

1. _____
   _____
2. _____
   _____
3. _____
   _____
4. _____
   _____

List and explain 4 reasons a parent may grant going out privileges.

1. _____
   _____
2. _____
   _____
3. _____
   _____
4. _____
   _____

How important is having going out privileges to you? Explain.

_____
_____
_____
_____
_____

Arguments in the Home

Are there arguments in your home?   Yes   No

Who starts most of the arguments in the home? Explain.

_____

_____

_____

What are most of the arguments in the home about? Explain.

_____

_____

_____

_____

_____

Do you contribute to the arguments in the home? Explain.

_____

_____

_____

_____

How can the arguments in the home be minimized? Explain.

_____

_____

_____

_____

Choose four of the words below and use each in a sentence to explain how the problems in the home may be minimized. (Listening, patience, honest, careful, think, responsible, act)

1. _____

_____

2. _____

_____

3. _____

_____

4. _____

_____

Neatness and Tidiness

Jessica, it has been three days since I asked you to organize your dresser and to remove the dishes from your bedroom floor. We have a problem with rodents so it is important that you keep your room clean.

Mom, I am not a child. I am 13 years old. I am not ready to clean my room. I will clean up after I return from Trisha's house.

By the way, I need $20.00 to pay my phone bill because it will be disconnected today.

Has Jessica's mother said anything wrong or spoken in a disrespectful manner to Jennifer?

Yes   No

Explain.

_____

_____

If you were Jessica's mother, how would you react in this situation? Explain.

_____

_____

_____

What are your suggestions to Jessica?

_____

_____

_____

Jessica's Situation

Write a letter to Jessica about her behavior. Tell Jessica your reaction to her behavior, how you feel her mother communicated to her, and about other sacrifices her mother may be making to take care of her. Finally, tell her, if you were her mother, how you would discipline her and then give her some recommendations about ways to improve her behaviors.

Dear Jessica,

_____

_____

_____

_____

_____

_____

_____

_____

_____

_____

_____

_____

_____

_____

_____

_____

_____

_____

_____

_____

_____

_____

_____

_____

_____

_____

_____

_____

_____

_____

Punishments

Do you get punished at home for engaging in negative behaviors?   Yes   No

When was the last time you were punished? Explain.

_____

_____

_____

_____

Who does the punishing in the home? _____

What were you punished for the last time you were punished? Explain.

_____

_____

_____

_____

Was the punishment fair or unfair? Explain.

_____

_____

_____

_____

If you were a parent, would you punish your children?   Yes   No

How would you punish your children? Explain.

_____

_____

_____

_____

Do you think that young people can benefit in the long run by being reprimanded or punished for being engaged in negative behaviors? Explain.

_____

_____

_____

_____

What bothers you most about being punished? Explain.

_____

_____

_____

_____

Interaction with the Police

Lionel is a 16-year-old old African American male. He was on his way home from school one day. At first he began walking, then he began running as soon as he remembered that his mother was going to work that evening and he had promised her to look after his younger brother. While running, he was pulled over by the police. They assumed that he had done something wrong and decided to stop him, then searched his pockets and his backpack. The police found nothing on him and he was told that he is free to go. Lionel felt violated because he felt like he was profiled because of his race.

If you were Lionel, how would you feel?

_____

_____

_____

_____

_____

If you were Lionel, would you continue to run after being asked to stop by the police? Explain.

_____

_____

_____

_____

_____

What about your decision in the above answer may be a good or bad idea? Explain.

_____

_____

_____

_____

Have you ever had a negative interaction with the police? Explain what happened.

_____

_____

_____

_____

_____

Curfew

Ron! There you go again. You are on probation, and you should be in the house at 9:30 pm. It is now 9:45 pm. I want this to be the last time you get home after 9:30.

Dad you are making a big deal out of nothing. I left Chris's house at 9:25. You know the bus takes 20 minutes to get here.

Yes, that's why should leave Chris' house at or before 9:00 so that you can get home on time.

It's not a big deal dad; you make a big thing out of the smallest thing.

Who is being unreasonable in the scenario? Explain.

_____

_____

How can the problem be solved? Explain.

_____

_____

Anger

Being angry is a normal feeling. However, the manner in which anger is expressed can be a problem.

Do you get angry easily?   Yes   No

Has anyone told you that you get angry easily?   Yes   No

Explain.

_____

_____

What makes you explode?

_____

_____

And how do you express yourself when you explode?

_____

_____

_____

What makes you mad?

_____

_____

And how do you express yourself when you are mad?

_____

_____

_____

What makes you frustrated?

_____

_____

And how do you express yourself when you are frustrated?

_____

_____

_____

What disappoints you?

_____

_____

And how do you express your disappointment?

_____

_____

_____

Anger Continued

Does the manner in which you express your anger make the situation better? Explain.

_____

_____

_____

_____

_____

_____

_____

How would you like to express your anger? Explain.

_____

_____

_____

_____

_____

List and explain five healthy ways in which people can express their anger. Here are some examples: Riding a bike, walking away from the situation, taking your mind to a peaceful place.

1. _____

_____

2. _____

_____

3. _____

_____

4. _____

_____

5. _____

_____

Challenges with Reading and Comprehending

Some young people experience difficulties reading and understanding, and this can trigger frustration, anger, and resentment.

Do you experience any difficulties in reading and understanding?   Yes   No

In what academic area/areas are you strong, meaning that you need no help or just a little help in that area? Explain.

_____

_____

_____

In what academic area/s are you weak, meaning you need a lot of help in that area in order to be successful? Explain.

_____

_____

_____

Does your difficulty in reading and understanding sometimes cause you to feel angry and mad? Explain.

_____

_____

_____

Does your frustration in reading cause you to take your anger out on others? Explain.

_____

_____

_____

Do you ever feel closed from the rest of the world because of the challenges you experience reading and understanding? Explain.

_____

_____

_____

How do you feel you can improve your reading skills?

_____

_____

_____

Difficulties in Reading and Understanding Continued

Joseph is a 15-year-old African American male. He is currently in foster care because of the severe behavioral problems he was displaying in the home setting. His parents were no longer able to manage his negative behaviors and as a result he was committed to the Department of Social Services. He was first placed in shelter care for two weeks, and then was transitioned to foster care. During Joseph's first session with the therapist, he shared that he experienced a lot of difficulties reading. He reports that it is very frustrating when his peers understand instructions in class and he doesn't. He further reports that he wants to learn, but is having difficulties grasping information the first time instructions are given. Additionally, he reports that in order for him to learn, he has to ask the teacher multiple questions. He claims that he is ashamed because his classmates make him feel like he is dumb. He claims that anything and everything makes him angry because he feels like he is "cut off" from the rest of the world. He reports that his difficulties in reading causes him to act out negatively at home, school and in the community.

Do you admire anything about Joseph's story? Explain.

_____

_____

_____

Is there anything about Joseph's story you can identify with? Explain.

_____

_____

_____

How can Joseph ask for help?

_____

_____

_____

What can Joseph do to resolve the problem with his family so that he may return to their placement? Explain.

_____

_____

_____

Help Joseph understand the reason his family had for having him placed in foster care. Explain.

_____

_____

_____

Sadness and Depression

Ricardo is a 16-year-old Hispanic male. His parents immigrated to the United States from Panama. They first lived in San Francisco, California. Two years ago, they relocated to Silver Springs, Maryland because the company that Ricardo's mother worked for gave her a promotion, and as a result she was required to relocate to the area. At first, Ricardo was very sad because it meant that he would be moving away from all his friends and the things he enjoyed in California. Ricardo particularly wanted to graduate from his high school in California. Initially when he moved to the Silver Springs area, he was reluctant to make new friends because he did not want to develop friendships just in case he had to move again. As time progressed, he became very close friends with a boy named Matt. Ricardo and Matt pretty much did everything together. Matt was super cool. One morning, Ricardo went to school and his classmates were all very sad. He asked what was happening, and was told that Matt was killed in a car crash by a drunk driver. Ricardo was emotionally devastated, and as the months prolonged, it became worse and worse. Ricardo refused to talk to anyone about his feelings. Several months later, Ricardo began to act out both at home and at school. He became disrespectful to his mother and teachers. In addition, he began using marijuana and came home way after the curfew established for him.

Have you ever engaged in negative activities because of feelings of sadness and depression?

Explain.

_____

_____

_____

Can you identify with Ricardo's story?   Yes   No

Explain.

_____

_____

_____

Have you ever lost a close friend or relative?   Yes   No

If yes, how did you cope or react to the loss?

_____

_____

_____

What suggestions, if any, do you have for Ricardo to help him cope with his problems?

_____

_____

_____

Incarceration of a Parent

Oftentimes inner city youths have to cope with a parent being incarcerated.

Is/are any of your parents currently incarcerated?   Yes   No

Has/have any of your parents been incarcerated in the past?   Yes   No

If a parent is incarcerated or was incarcerated, which parent is or was incarcerated?

_____

How long was this person incarcerated or how long will this person be incarcerated?

_____

You may not be comfortable talking about the reason for your parent's incarceration. If you are not comfortable, move on to the next question. If you are comfortable, explain your understanding of the reason for your parent's incarceration.

_____
_____
_____
_____

How has this incarceration affected you? Explain.

_____
_____
_____
_____

How has this incarceration affected your family? Explain.

_____
_____
_____
_____

Are you able, or were you able to visit this incarcerated parent? Explain.

_____
_____
_____
_____

Has your feelings or respect for this parent changed after the incarceration? Explain.

_____
_____
_____
_____

Substance Abuse by a Parent or Caregiver

Do any of your parents use illicit substances? (marijuana, cocaine, heroin) Name the parent and the substance he or she uses.

_____

_____

_____

_____

Does your parent's substance abuse affect your relationship with this parent?   Yes   No

Explain how this parent's substance use affects your relationship with him or her.

_____

_____

_____

_____

Do you ever experience any fear about your parent's life or safety because of his or her substance use? Explain.

_____

_____

_____

_____

How does your parent's substance use disrupt/affect the family?

_____

_____

_____

_____

Do you experience any feelings of shame or embarrassment because of your parent's substance use? Explain.

_____

_____

_____

_____

In your opinion, what can this person do to fix the problem? Explain.

_____

_____

_____

_____

_____

Housing

Some inner city youths experience challenges with stable and adequate housing.

Does your family experience any problems with stable housing?   Yes   No

Does your family experience any problems with adequate housing?   Yes   No

What, if any, has been the housing problem/s experienced by your family?

Explain.

_____
_____
_____

How does your family's housing problems affect your:

Emotions:

_____
_____
_____

Education:

_____
_____
_____

Safety:

_____
_____
_____

Health:

_____
_____
_____

Friendships:

_____
_____
_____

Running Away from Home

Have you ever ran away from home?   Yes   No

Have you ever thought of running away from where you currently live?   Yes   No

If you ran away from your home or current residence in the past, what happened that caused you to run away? Explain.

_____

_____

_____

The last time you ran away, where did you go? Explain.

_____

_____

_____

What was your experience like at the place or places you stayed while you were away from your family? Explain.

_____

_____

_____

What kind of activities were you engaged in while you were away from your family? Explain.

_____

_____

_____

Did/do you have any regrets about running away from your home? Explain.

_____

_____

_____

Did you return to the home you ran away from?   Yes   No

If yes, what made you return to the home? Explain.

_____

_____

_____

What do you think needs to happen in your home to prevent you from repeating that behavior? Explain.

_____

_____

_____

Self Esteem

On the scale below, rate your self-esteem with 1 being the lowest and 10 being the highest.

_____

1   2   3   4   5   6   7   8   9   10

What does high self-esteem mean to you?

_____
_____
_____
_____

In your own words, how might low self-esteem affect young people?

_____
_____
_____
_____

What do you think might contribute to low self-esteem?

_____
_____
_____
_____

Do you know of anyone, including yourself, who may be experiencing low self-esteem?

Yes   No

If yes, explain.

_____
_____
_____
_____

What can this person do to help him or her build good self-esteem?

_____
_____
_____
_____

True False

1. As children get older, the nature of the challenges they present oftentimes change.
    True   False   Unsure

2. As children get older, parents are usually better equipped to deal with their behavioral problems. True   False   Unsure

3. Parents are never uncomfortable talking to their children and teenagers about any problem. True   False   Unsure

4. Peer pressure is always negative and can never be positive. True   False   Unsure

5. Young people oftentimes show symptoms of depression which are different from symptoms presented by adults, and their engagement in negative behaviors can be a sign of depression. True   False   Unsure

6. Marijuana can distort people's thought process and may affect their relationship with family members and their performance at school. True   False   Unsure

7. Victims of robberies oftentimes feel violated. True   False   Unsure

8. Animal cruelty is a strong predictor of future negative behaviors. True   False   Unsure

9. Gun violence is a problem which only occurs in inner city neighborhoods.
    True   False   Unsure

10. Selling drugs is always a risky activity. True   False   Unsure

11. Young people in inner city neighborhoods oftentimes have more difficulties interacting with the police and other law enforcement officials. True   False   Unsure

12. Having structure and discipline at home and at school is a good predictor of future success. True   False   Unsure

13. Unstable and inadequate housing is never a problem for young people.
    True   False   Unsure

14. Just because someone is shy, it does not mean that he/she has low self-esteem.
    True   False   Unsure

Future Career/Occupation

It is quite usual for young people from across the world to begin thinking about their future career or profession by age 13.

Has anyone in your family ever asked you about your future career?   Yes   No

Who asked you and what did this person ask?

_____

_____

_____

_____

If someone asked about your career, how did that make you feel?

_____

_____

_____

_____

Is there anyone in your family whom you expected to ask you about your future career and that person never asked? How did/does that make you feel?

_____

_____

_____

_____

What career or profession interests you? Explain what interests you about this career or profession.

_____

_____

_____

_____

What can you do now to help you prepare for that career or profession?

_____

_____

_____

_____

How might this career change you and your family's life?

_____

_____

_____

_____

Future Life

In the box below draw a picture of how your future life would be, or get picture from a magazine newspaper or the internet to visually depict your future life.

What do you like about this drawing or collage?

_____

_____

_____

_____

_____

_____